I Just Wanna Be Free

My Life. My Words. My Testimony.

Latashia Renee

Copyright © 2020 by Latashia Renee

Unless otherwise indicated, all scripture quotations are from the Holy Bible, NEW KING JAMES VERSION. All rights reserved.

No part of this book may be reproduced, distributed, or transmitted in any form or by any means, without prior written permission of the author.

Second Edition: October 2022

Author's Note: This work is a memoir. Events, actions and their consequences over a period of time have been retold as the author presently remembers them. Some names and identifying details have been changed to protect the privacy of those involved, and some dialogue has been re-created from memory. Some scenes are composites of events, and the timeline for some events have been compressed.

Library of Congress Cataloging-in-Publications Data
Latashia Renee

I Just Wanna Be Free: My Life. My Words. My Testimony.
Printed in the United States of America

ISBN-9798663745000

For every woman, young or old, who dares to fight back and take your rightful place in Christ.

For those of you who will have the audacity to trust again, hope again, and love again…

This book is for you.

Foreword

MORE THAN A CONQUEROR... Latashia Renee is a true example of Paul's words in *Romans 8:37*! Through these pages Latashia has laid her life out as portrait for all of us to see that, in Christ, we are able to not only face our problems and issues but to overcome. She has not only survived, but is now thriving in areas where she could have accepted defeat. She is boldly determined to share her story so that others will be encouraged and inspired. She walks in an integrity and transparency that is almost unreal in a world full of fake and phony. She is her writing and you will clearly see that her grace, poise and professionalism exudes from the pages.

As a pastor, author, and Transformational Coach I have many opportunities to interact with people who hide and cover up their past and present conditions of abuse, addictions, rejection, failed marriages, unwanted diagnosis, and so on. Not Latashia. She is fearless as she performs a chronological walk through her life, including all the chaos and pain that she has endured. Her writing style is so intentional that as a reader you feel as if you are standing right there with her as she experiences tragedies and triumphs that many face but refuse to address. Her ability to break out of bondage more than once and maneuver into her freedom will leave you empowered. Not such a rose-colored life but it's her truth and she shares vivid details that will often mirror truths that we have faced as well! Her sense of humor, a personality trait that is so rare for a person who has had this much trauma in their life, is sprinkled throughout and will often give you comfort in knowing that trouble don't last always.

I had the pleasure of coaching Latashia as she finished this body of work. A few times it honestly got challenging because "Freedom" can be obtained but maintaining it is another process. Freedom is also done in layers, so even when we peel back one layer there's always another behind it. Latashia's commitment to others both personally and through her ministry was never the issue. Her commitment to fully put herself first was often lacking. After our sessions, her boldness went to another level, she became uncompromising and unashamed to fully write from a new perspective... one that was completely healed because areas that had been ignored have now been conquered. As my spiritual daughter, I saw true transformation in her life. After reading her book, I can fully validate that this is written not just from observation but experience. Experience that yields principles that assist and give guidance to our lives as well as others. Through her experience her readers have a guide that challenges and comforts them through their process if they are willing to do the work.

"I Just Wanna Be Free" is not only a statement. It is a bold declaration that resembles a decision that we all will or have to make at some point especially in our spiritual walk. It is also a prayer that is translated from our spirits to God when we have had enough of the bondage in our lives whether self-inflicted or forced on us by others. This book

will challenge you to acknowledge and face your personal "Goliaths" and like David go in for the kill! Your spirit will be challenged to arise and accept no less than a victory over your marred past and recognize that it was never God's intent for you to walk in shame but in triumph in every area of your life. This book is not for the faint hearted, nor the half - hearted but the whole-hearted who are ready to work on not only obtaining your freedom but maintaining it. Hopefully your freedom will challenge you to do the same as Latashia - to tell your truth that it may help others!

This book will add value to your library and offer you a great resource and reference to helping others during their process.

Pastor Orienthia Speakman

CEO & Founder of SpeakO Worldwide Ministry

Contents

INTRODUCTION: TELL THE TRUTH 9
1 BONNIE & CLYDE 14
2 THE INTERRUPTION OF EVERYTHING 20
3 TSUNAMI OF PAIN 33
4 WHY DID I GET MARRIED? 43
5 THE STRUGGLE IS REAL 54
6 BEAUTY FOR ASHES 64
7 FREE INDEED 73
ABOUT THE AUTHOR 87

"Our deepest fear is not that we are inadequate. Our deepest fear is that we are powerful beyond measure. It is our light, not our darkness that most frightens us. We ask ourselves, who am I to be brilliant, gorgeous, talented, fabulous? Actually, who are you not to be? You are a child of God. Your playing small does not serve the world. There is nothing enlightened about shrinking so that other people won't feel insecure around you. We are all meant to shine, as children do. We were born to make manifest the glory of God that is within us. It's not just in some of us; it's in everyone. And as we let our own light shine, we unconsciously give other people permission to do the same. As we are liberated from our own fear, our presence automatically liberates others."

Marianne Williamson

INTRODUCTION: TELL THE TRUTH

And ye shall know the truth, and the truth shall make you free.

John 8:32 (KJV)

"**NO!**" It was a simple answer. But it wasn't the one my teacher was expecting. She was worried. Others seemed frantic. The ambulance was on the way.

I was bent over with both arms wrapped around myself, rocking back and forth, trying to ease the pain. There was blood everywhere. I tried to clean up the mess before anyone could see, but I couldn't. The pain was much too unbearable.

My teacher asked a question with a seemingly obvious answer, "Latashia, do you want me to call your mother?"

I looked at her with tears flooding from my eyes, and said "No!"

She looked at me with a puzzled expression. Surely, I must have misunderstood the question. When she asked me a second time, she touched my shoulder to make sure she had my full attention.

My answer remained the same.

"Please don't call my mama." I whimpered.

"I'll be fine" as I heard the sirens getting louder and louder.

❖

I recently told a close friend that I was going to finally tell my story. She said she was nervous for me. I told her I was afraid. Like, *really* afraid!

I just kept thinking about how my past is filled with so much disobedience, chaos, crooked paths, and filthy secrets. The truth is, I have been a prisoner of my own shame and humiliation for as long as I can remember. I knew I would be taking a huge risk by unloading my dirty laundry. The risk is you'll judge me, treat me differently; even question my salvation. Maybe that's why it took so long for me to put it all on paper for the world to read. But somewhere between my fear and my desperate cries for freedom I decided it was worth it. YOU were worth it.

I have written and "finished" this book many times. I even submitted the manuscript once to a publishing company in Washington and it was accepted. To say I was excited would be an understatement. I felt so accomplished. My dream was finally coming true. I began to think about all the lives that would be touched by my story and all the new places I would go. But then I got scared and I decided my story wasn't good enough to be shared. Or rather, I wasn't good enough. So, I retreated and let my dream slip through my fingers.

That was almost seven years ago.

Looking back, I was just not ready. There was still so much more that God needed to teach me and so many more things I needed to overcome and surrender. Back then, I was living a lie; dancing around my issues and hiding my truth. You deserve better than that.

God has a way of teaching us so many lessons; if only we would stop and take notice. For most of my life, I didn't pay attention to the cues. I simply floated through life thinking "whatever happens, happens." I accepted the blows and gut punches that came and I never thought to fight back. Even after I received Christ and began ministering to others, I still did not consistently apply the Word of God to my life. I had a "form of godliness" (according to *2 Timothy 3:5*) in public, but my personal life was a wreck. I loved God and had a sincere desire to live for Him, but my brokenness was in the way. I had been through so much and I refused to surrender my pain to God. I guess, you can call it pure stubbornness. As time passed and my life became more chaotic, the Holy Spirit began tugging at my very core; a familiar feeling I had as a lost teenager. It was attached to the prayer I prayed while riding in the back of an ambulance at just 18 years old. My prayer was 5 simple words: **"I Just Wanna Be Free."**

A year later while standing at the foot of my bed, the Lord reminded me again of my prayer. He told me that would be the title of my first book. Although writing was my passion, I had never considered becoming an author. And I certainly couldn't imagine penning such intimate details of my life. Those words were my cry for help! Those words would reveal the nights I had cried myself to sleep because of the things that were going on in my young mind. Penning the life surrounding those 5 words would unleash a flood of emotions, and I wasn't sure I was ready for that. So, I continued to suffer in silence, not trusting even God; believing my thoughts, fears, and pain never really mattered. I covered my suffering with a mask of strength, while battling every storm I encountered alone. It was all so simple to me. I just wanted those closest to me to be proud of me, to support me, to love me, at ANY cost…even if it meant being something or someone who I wasn't. Now I see I was living a life of bondage. Sadly, this behavior followed me into adulthood as well.

My entire life seems to have been one big masquerade, a real-life soap opera so to speak. Only I, the lead actress, never bothered to show up. I should have 5 or 6 Oscars for the type of performances I've put on over the years. It's nothing to be proud of though. I've lost a lot of good people because of my unwillingness to be authentic. That's no way to live. It gets old and lonely. I had to lose everything and everybody for me to take a long, hard look in the mirror and deal with my issues head on. It was after my "mirror moment" that I would truly surrender to the call of God on my life and be obedient to His plan. I decided to come clean and release my dark and painful past. I had to do this if I wanted to minister in truth to women who were bound by their past and felt as if God could never use them.

Let me warn you, you're going to read some things that may shock, disappoint, and most definitely anger you. I get it. But hang in there with me and keep reading. Now I can finally obey God and tell the whole truth. Besides, folks have heard enough lies.

I haven't experienced everything, but I have certainly experienced enough to comfort you with these words, "you are not alone and you are never too far gone." When I began my journey to freedom, I didn't understand there would be sacrifices, tears, and many "valley" experiences. Even so, I don't regret anything because I learned that God is not wasteful. He uses every mistake, wrong turn, and failure as an opportunity to show Himself strong and mighty in our lives. The Bible says in *Romans 8:28, "And we know that all things work together for good to those who love God, to those who are the called according to His purpose."* God is very strategic in His works. Our own fear is what hinders us in His purpose for us.

Fear has often stood for; **F**orget **E**verything **A**nd **R**un.

Well, I'm tired of running.

Aren't you?

LATASHIA RENEE

1 BONNIE & CLYDE

The best thing about having a sister was that I always had a friend.

~Cali Rae Turner

Growing up, I was never much of a leader. My sister was 22 months older than me and had enough leadership skills for the both of us. Even as a young child, she was a dare devil who wasn't afraid of anything. Because I wanted to be just like her, I did everything she told me to do and everything I saw her do.

I have so many vivid childhood memories of the two of us. Some incredibly funny, and others that make me want to punch myself for listening to her.

When my sister and I were very young, perhaps 3 and 5 years old we each received a Big Wheel for Christmas. This was around 1985 and a Big Wheel was considered the toy of Champions. We would drive at top speed down our long driveway doing all kinds of little tricks. This was an everyday thing for us. On one of those days my sister decided she was tired of just riding up and down our driveway. She wanted to go to White Lake Water Park, which was about 5 miles from our home.

I JUST WANNA BE FREE

She looked at me and said, "Come on Tashia. Let's go"

We hopped on our Big Wheel and off we went. We pedaled down our driveway, turned on our imaginary signal lights riding to what we thought would be tons of fun. We managed to get about 4 houses down the street before we were spotted by one of our neighbors, who drove us home, but not before scolding us for playing in the road. She told us to behave, then she left.

Our mama worked third shift and was asleep, totally unaware of our antics. We waited a short while; long enough until my sister thought it was safe to leave out again. We jumped on our Big Wheels again, pedaling as fast as we could past the neighbor's house as to not be seen.

Whew! We made it all the way to the end of the road (at least a mile) and we were excited to be on our way for a fun filled day. We approached the stop sign, and sat side by side while we each looked both ways before "driving" onto Hwy 701.

Did I mention we were only 3 and 5 years old?

Hwy 701 was an extremely busy 2 lane road, often travelled by 18- wheeler tractor trailer trucks traveling from one town to another.

As we looked to our left, we saw the truck but it seemed so far away. My sister said we could make the turn. So of course, we did. We must've only gotten a fourth of a block before we realized we were holding up traffic. Much to our surprise, the 18-wheeler truck had caught up to us and was now behind us frantically blowing the horn. Surely, the driver was trying to get the attention of an adult to alarm them that there were children in the middle of the highway.

Instead of us moving out of traffic, my sister and I just kept pedaling on down the road. We even paused briefly to turn around and wave at the trucker and encouraged him to continue blowing his horn by moving our arms up and down. (This story is hilarious now.) Our cousin Eddie was in his house but heard the commotion and ran and got us out of the road. He picked us up like we were little rag dolls and threw our Big Wheels on the back of his truck. I knew we had really messed up this time. I had never seen Eddie so angry. When he finally calmed down, he began asking questions like,

"What were you girls thinking?"

"Where were you going?"

"Where is Pam?"

My sister answered his questions confidently.

"We were bored and wanted to have some fun. We were going to White Lake. And mama is sleep!"

She was so fearless. I, on the other hand, was not! I knew once Eddie took us home, we were in for the worst whooping of our lives. Boy, was I right! As soon as Eddie told our mama what happened, she gave us a good old-fashioned butt whooping that I never forgot. Mama went back to sleep, but not before warning us what would happen if we went back outside. But when she woke up, she whooped us AGAIN! I guess she had more time to think about our actions and got mad (or scared) all over again. Mama knew things could have turned out very differently for us that day. I knew even at 3 years old we had crossed the line big time.

I JUST WANNA BE FREE

The fear of our mother's wrath didn't last long in my sister's eyes because a short while later, we were at it again. By this time, she and I were a little older. Our mama has always been a smoker, so there were always cigarettes in our house. My sister convinced me that smoking was the cool thing to do. So, she stole a cigarette and we headed outside to "smoke." My mama drove a 1982 Plymouth Champ, the hatchback version. It was a small, brown ugly little car. But it was big enough for my sister and me to crouch down in the front on the floor. She was on the driver side. I was on the passenger side.

Having a ball.

Laughing.

Smoking.

Coughing.

Choking.

Mama must've heard us (or perhaps saw the smoke coming out of the windows) because just a few moments later she was yanking us out of the car and beating our behinds.

Yet another whooping I received at the expense of my older sister.

Then there is the banana pudding incident. Mama baked banana pudding for dessert. When she went to sleep, I ate it all. Besides, my sister said I could. It was so good, but it made me extremely sick. I ended up vomiting all over my mama's new bedroom curtains and when she found out, I thought she was going to beat the black off me.

And guess what?

I've never eaten banana pudding since.

Ever.

These are the stories that are always told at family functions when my mama and aunts are trying to convince others that my sister and I were bad kids. We were the modern-day Bonnie and Clyde; well minus the killing and stealing. We stayed in trouble!

But what did they expect? My sister and I did everything together. We played together. Fought together. Bathed together. We wore our hair the same. We wore matching clothes. Heck, most people may have thought we were twins if I was thinner and had a darker skin complexion. When you saw one, you saw the other. We were inseparable. Our names are even similar. Her name is "La'Shondria Dene." The legal spelling of my name is "La'Tashia Rene." And our younger sister's name (who is 5 years my junior) is "La'Deidra Jene." I suppose my mama loved the letters "La" followed by an apostrophe, and middle names that rhymed. We all have different last names also, even though my older sister and I have both the same parents. The explanation of that is quite complicated. Let's just say my mama was very strategic when it came to naming her children. I never really cared for the apostrophe and additional capitalization in my name. It seemed a bit too complex, so I made a few adjustments. As to not confuse others, we were typically identified by our nicknames: Poggie, Tashia, and Deidra.

I JUST WANNA BE FREE

We loved our mama, but we were all daddy's girls. My biological father was sentenced to 50 years in prison when I was an infant. As a result, my mother moved away and met someone else, "Woodrow Wilson Underwood." He was named after the 28th President of the United States of America. But everyone called him either "Reiny" or "Underwood." He soon became my "daddy" and he was the best thing since sliced bread. He treated my older sister and me as if we were his biological children. His sisters and brother became our aunts and uncle. His parents became our grandparents. He was good to us and spoiled us rotten! My mama was definitely the disciplinarian. He was the provider. He brought balance and stability. If he ever had to discipline us, it was a last resort. He'd keep us in line with a pinch. Trust me, we would rather have gotten a whooping from our mama. Those pinches hurt!

In the beginning, it was just Poggie and me. Daddy's girls. Then he and my mama decided they wanted another child. On October 11, 1987, Deidra joined our family. She was supposed to be a boy. Mama had her name already picked out, La'Dedrick Denard. I think Reiny really wanted a boy too, but you couldn't tell by how he treated her. He loved her and spoiled her just like he did with Poggie and me. He never shunned us nor made us feel as if we were no longer his children just because he finally had a biological child.

He was such an excellent example and role model for all of us. He wasn't perfect; just what we needed. My mama and he had a rocky relationship and they eventually split up. He remained present in our lives though; just a phone call away. He took care of us, no matter what.

2 THE INTERRUPTION OF EVERYTHING

It hurts until it doesn't. You think it's going to break you, but it won't. You might not sleep as well at night, but you will be fine. Numb. But numb and fine are the same.

~Mellie Grant, Scandal

After mama and Reiny broke up, my mom moved my sisters and me to the next county over. Even as children, we felt the hit of our parents separating. During this time, we moved A LOT. I am not sure why, but I can recall at least 6 different places we lived before I was in the 5th grade. Mama was suddenly angry all the time. Her fuse was short. She seemed to always be yelling and screaming at us over the smallest little things. I'd often wonder if she even wanted children or if she even loved the three of us.

Once a neighbor called Child Protective Services and reported a case of abuse and neglect against my mama. The report stated she was mistreating us and leaving us home alone while she hung out at night. To be honest, the report was true. She did do those things and a lot more. But we loved our mama and did not want to be removed from her custody. Even though we were children, my older sister and I knew the day would come when our mama would have to address the case against her. We were not surprised when we saw the white Department of Social Services vehicle pull into our driveway a few weeks later. Even at 10 and 12 years old, we knew the man was coming to take us away. However, we had no intention of going anywhere with him. We snuck out the back door and ran down the street to a neighbor's house and called our mama. (Ironically, it was the same neighbor who reported the case). We were safe, so we thought. But it didn't take long for the man to find us and take us back home. By then, our mama was home and she was furious! She told us to get out of the car and go in the house because we were not going anywhere with him if she could help it.

As my sister and I stood with our faces pressed against the window eavesdropping, we could hear our mama screaming and cussing that man out. It may sound crazy, but in that moment, I was so proud to be her daughter. She wasn't perfect, but she was fighting for us! She wasn't just going to turn us over to DSS without a fight. And that *had* to mean she really did love us. She told him if he or anyone else from Child Protective Services ever stepped foot back on her property again she would…well, I can't tell y'all EVERYTHING! But let's just say, we never heard from them again.

Over time my older sister and I grew apart. We were no longer thick as thieves. She was suddenly angry too. It was as if she woke up one day and didn't like me anymore. Suddenly, I was her enemy. She had become a bully and I was her primary target. She and mama were always fighting, yelling, and screaming at each other. The atmosphere at home had become hostile. And on top of all of that, she began accusing me of thinking I was better than her. I was dumbfounded by her accusation. Who me, think I was better than her? We were kids! Moreover, we were sisters!

Honestly, I wanted to be just like her. Not the tyrant she had become, but the person she was at her core. The brave, strong, resilient, dare devil. Her! I wanted to be THAT person. I didn't understand what was happening, but I felt it was best to separate myself from it all. It was obvious to me that the Bonnie & Clyde duo had been dismantled. From that moment, I became a total recluse. It was during this time that I developed my love for reading and writing. I quickly learned I could escape from the Land of Evil & Chaos by entering the lives of the girls from "The Babysitters Club" or the students in "The Sweet Valley High" novels. I would spend hours at a time doing absolutely nothing but reading book after book. Anything to take my mind off the dysfunction going on around me. They had their way of handling things, and well, I had mine.

Let me pause for a moment and say this: Hindsight is always 20/20 so I know now this was a defense mechanism; my way of coping with the rejection I was feeling. Up to that moment, I always felt loved, safe, and secure. Suddenly I had to create ways to hide, smother, or bury my feelings without ever addressing them head on. I began asking myself, "Is something wrong with me?" or

"Is this my fault?" Yet again, "Did I do something wrong?"

All this alone time was an opportunity for my mind to wander. I begin to think about my biological father. I only knew three things about him. His name was Willie Edward Cole, Jr., he was in prison, and he used to physically abuse my mother. I was supposed to hate him or at least feel indifferent towards him, but I didn't. I didn't think about him at all. I had Reiny so I had no reason to think about anyone else.

I wasn't trying to be ungrateful. I appreciated the fact that Reiny was there. But I couldn't stop that yearning in the pit of my stomach either. I wanted to meet my biological father. I wanted to get to know him. I didn't want to offend or replace Reiny, I just had so many questions. Who was he? What was he like? What were his parents like? Where did my big jaws and high cheek bones come from? I felt as if a piece of my life was missing. I needed answers. But my mama hated him. I knew she would never allow us to visit him. He often wrote to my sister and me but I needed more. I wanted to look at him face to face.

I needed to understand who I was and where I came from.

Quite frankly, I was a good kid. I was smart, responsible, and respectful. I had two flaws that my oldest sister always reminded me of. I was lazy and I was naïve. She would say this when she would get in one of her rages and decide to yell, scream, and pick at me. I can admit now that she was right. I was lazy and in fact very naïve. My oldest sister used to say I had plenty of book smarts but not a lick of common sense, or "street smarts" as she called it. But, at my age, why did I need "street smarts?" I thought the world was a safe place and people didn't just hurt others simply because they could. Unlike her, I enjoyed living a sheltered life and other than my chaotic home life, I was genuinely happy.

That is, until my happiness was abruptly interrupted….

Things changed for me the summer of 1994. I was going into the 7th grade and my mama let me spend the night with one of my classmates. I had stayed over there a few times before. I never really did much more than watch TV and read books at her house. Sometimes even that was hard to do because her mother always had people coming in and out of her house. One such person was this guy who would always stop by their house when I visited. His name was Ricky. We'd always laugh and joke when he'd come to the house.

He was 25 years old and the finest man I had ever seen in my entire life. I was completely mesmerized the very first time I laid eyes on him….and he knew it! I wasn't sure how he knew, but he did. So, to play it off, I started being very mean to him whenever I had to be in his presence. I would roll my eyes and suck my teeth at him every chance I got. But after a while, I realized my disdain had become attractive to him; and I didn't know how to deal with that. He started flirting with me and always wanted to "hang out" with me. I was so confused because I couldn't figure out why this 25-year-old man wanted to spend so much time with me when he could be with people his own age. But I thought, "What the heck!" Besides, I did enjoy the attention. It wasn't as if anyone else was paying me much attention anyway. He would always tell me how pretty and smart he thought I was. I began to look forward to seeing him...just so I could hear more compliments.

One day while I was visiting my friend, he poured cold water on my face while I was asleep in the living room. He said he was trying to wake me up, but I didn't care. I couldn't stand the sight of him anymore! It was weeks before I ever went back to spend the night at my friend's house again.

The next time I went back would prove to be my last night ever stepping foot back in my friend's house. When I saw him again, I was in my friend's bedroom reading a book. He came in and said he wanted to talk. Had I been a bit wiser I would have immediately known what he really came in the room to do was to seduce me. At first, we did talk, of course after he apologized pouring the water on me. We talked about random stuff like my family, my grades in school, and what I wanted to be when I grew up. I could barely contain my excitement when I told him I wanted to be a school teacher, then maybe later a principal. He really had my attention because it seemed as if everything about me suddenly mattered to him. I was flattered because of course I was just happy somebody, anybody was showing me some attention. We continued to laugh and talk for a little while more, before he said he had to leave, but he would be back later.

I nonchalantly said, "okay."

Disclaimer: What you are about to read may be difficult,

I JUST WANNA BE FREE

as the details are extremely disturbing and graphic. Please take that into account before you continue.

I must have fallen asleep because the next thing I remember were my friend's pit bulls outside barking and Ricky knocking on my friend's bedroom window. I quietly opened the window and let him in so the dogs would shut up. He came in through the window and began talking to me but I was so sleepy that I could barely keep up with the conversation. So, I crawled back into bed, but he got in with me. At first I thought I was imagining things, but then he started to touch me all over my body.

Hold up.

Am I dreaming? This was NOT happening to me!

He wasn't kind and gentle at all. His mouth was all over me, on my neck, on my breasts, on my stomach, on the inside of my thighs, then….there. Everything was happening so fast. When I realized what he was doing to me, I almost threw up. I felt cheap, degraded, and the exact opposite of pleasure. He didn't seem to care at all. When he finally came up and I could see his face, his expression told me exactly what was about to happen next.

"Tashia, WAKE UP!"

"Please Tashia, YOU GOTTA WAKE UP!!!!!!!!!" I screamed to myself in silence.

But things were happening so quickly. It felt as if my body was being ripped in half, like my organs, tissues, and muscles were being yanked out of me all at once. The pain erupting from every place in my body told me this was NOT a dream.

This was really happening to me.

I started to panic.

I began kicking, screaming, and hitting him in his face, his arms, his chest, everywhere! I wanted him to get off of me! But he didn't budge. Instead, he picked up a pillow, pressed it against my face, and started smothering me with it. I thought, Oh God. He is going to kill me. I was struggling to breathe. My fight intensified. Even with the pillow covering my face, I screamed and fought harder and harder for him to get off of me.

I just kept thinking, Please God don't let him kill me! I am just a little girl and I don't want to die like this.

At some point, he leaned over and whispered, "Shut up!" His voice was so calm. Eerily calm. It was at that moment I realized fighting Ricky was useless. So, I stopped kicking and screaming and just laid very still. I didn't know what else to do.

I just knew my friend or her parents would burst in the room at any moment.

Why didn't they hear me screaming?

Couldn't they hear the headboard banging against the wall?

Where were they?

But no one ever came to save me.

I don't know how long the whole ordeal lasted because at some point I forced myself to think about something else. When I realized he was done, he was fully clothed and walking out of the room. He didn't go back out the window as he entered. I heard him walk right out the back door as if he lived there.

I was afraid to breathe or move. I laid there, staring at the ceiling for what seemed to be an eternity before I attempted to get up. My legs were so heavy they felt numb. Somehow, I found the strength to drag myself to the bathroom using the wall to hold myself up. I started to pee and I felt like I was on fire! I realized I was also bleeding. Still, I didn't bother bathing, because I was scared it would make me hurt even more.

By the time I got back to the bed, I was crying uncontrollably. I knew I wasn't an innocent little girl anymore. I had always been labeled as the smart one, but at that moment I felt stupid! My life had been interrupted. I had been robbed and life as I knew it, had officially changed.

And how could I explain to my friend (or anyone) what just happened? Surely, they would ask how Ricky got in the house. I had helped him climb in through the window, so that made it all my fault!

Or, so I believed.

Let me pause for a moment and say this: Rape is never the victim's fault. I don't care what the circumstances were leading up to the incident, what the victim was wearing, etc. NO MEANS NO!

As victims, we often blame ourselves, carrying the shame and humiliation that is attached to being violated. That, my dear sister, is a trick of the enemy. He wants to rob us twice. First of our innocence, then of our victory. The shame doesn't belong to the victim, it belongs to the attacker.

After months of pleading, mama finally let me and my older sister visit our biological father at Harnett County Correctional Center in Lillington, NC. By then it didn't matter to me anymore. I was angry at my daddy. I was angry at the world. Nothing made me happy and nothing made the anger go away.

I didn't know him, but I knew he should have been there to protect me and he wasn't. I vaguely remember our meeting. I know what I was wearing and the awkwardness that I felt, but that's about it. I didn't care who he was or who his parents were. I didn't want anything to do with him.

There I was trying to deal with being raped all alone, not knowing who to trust or who to tell. My daddy was in prison. My mama was distracted. And my older sister hated me. So, I completely shut down. I was always relatively quiet, so no one even noticed. I spent more and more time alone in my room. At school, while I made excellent grades, I was mean and disrespectful. I was disrespectful to my peers as well as my teachers. In-School-Suspension was a regular routine for me, which was supposed to be a punishment. However, they couldn't punish me any worse than I was already punishing myself. When my principal would tell me I'd have three days of ISS, and I'd simply say, "okay, whatever."

This went on for months.

No one noticed the changes in my behavior, until one day my technology teacher asked me to stay after the class dismissed.

Latashia, are you okay?

Yes.

Is everything okay at home?

Yes.

Is someone hurting you?

No.

Latashia, if someone has hurt you, you can tell me. I promise I will help you.

And then the dam broke. *Finally! Finally, someone could see I was NOT okay.*

I told her about Ricky. I told her how I let him in through the window. I told her how he raped me and how I thought he was going to kill me. I told her how nobody came to save me even though I screamed as loudly as I could. I told her how alone I felt. I told her I felt stupid and it was all my fault.

I cried. And cried. And cried.

She cried too.

She said she would have to tell the school principal and together they would get me some help. I didn't care who knew, I just wanted to be free!

Ms. Johnston, the principal, was never my favorite person. As I sat across from her as she listened to my teacher repeat what I had shared with her, she seemed human, like she had a heart. As if, she cared. When my teacher finished telling her my story, Ms. Johnston turned to me and with compassion in her eyes she said, "Latashia, we can handle this one of two ways. Either I can report this to the Department of Social Services and have Child Protective Services get involved, or you can go home today and tell your mother and I will let you deal with it as a family."

I chose the latter. Surely, involving DSS would be unwise. She said she wanted me to report back to her office the next morning and tell her what happened.

I agreed.

On the way home, I knew it would be difficult to tell my mama what happened to me. I also knew it was something I needed to do if I was ever going to get any help.

I walked into her bedroom that night prepared to tell her everything. She was sitting on the bed. I walked in and sat down near the foot of the bed with my back to her. We were both facing her television but I could tell her eyes were focused on me, not the television. I opened my mouth, but no words escaped. I cleared my throat. Still, nothing. I sat there thinking about the consequences if I told her I had been raped. I never doubted whether she would believe me. I knew she would. But I also knew she would find Ricky and cause bodily harm to him, or something worse. I couldn't be held responsible for her actions. So, I stood up, walked out of her bedroom, and never looked back.

The next day, Ms. Johnston asked me if I had talked to my mama. I told her yes. But that was a lie. I never said one word to her. I guess my response satisfied her, because we never spoke of it again.

From then on, I tried my best to pretend as if everything was okay. But it wasn't. No matter how much I laughed and smiled, I was lost and empty.

So, Mellie Grant is wrong. Numb and fine are not the same. Before my parents split up, I was fine. Before I lost my best friend (sister), I was fine. Before I was violently raped, I was fine. I didn't have to pretend to be. I didn't have to fake a smile, when I was really dying inside. I didn't have to cry myself to sleep at night.

Because I WAS FINE!

But now, I was just numb.

LATASHIA RENEE

3 TSUNAMI OF PAIN

Promise me you'll always remember: You're braver than you believe, stronger than you seem, and smarter than you think.

~*Winnie the Pooh to Christopher Robin*

By the time I got to high school, the depression, rejection, and abandonment I felt only magnified. I had become very promiscuous. Not because I wanted to be but because I was afraid to say "No." I didn't enjoy sex at all but I vowed not to ever be raped again. Ever! So, if that meant giving my body away to anyone who wanted it, then so be it. Maybe if I had not lied about talking to my mama I could have gotten the help that I needed. But I didn't, so I felt I had to suffer the consequences.

Over time, I'd become apathetic and angry. I was imploding but no one noticed. I continued to do well in school and continued to act normal, but I was far from normal. I was a ticking bomb.

One of my biggest sources of pain was my relationship with my mama. There was an incident that I don't think I will ever forget. My mama was cooking dinner one day and asked me to watch the food because she needed to step out. I agreed, but soon after she left, I fell asleep. I woke up to the smell of burned chicken and rice. The kitchen was completely filled with smoke. I panicked and was unsure what to do. I opened the windows to try to get the smoke out, then refilled the pot with water and put it back on the stove thinking my mama would be none the wiser.

Boy was I wrong!

When she returned home and realized our dinner was ruined, she was livid! She cussed me out like I was a man in the streets. I had to be about 15 when this happened. In between the cuss words, she said things like, "you're sorry, you're lazy, you make me sick, you ain't good for nothing!" I was helpless to defend myself against her rage. The entire time she was screaming at me, I just kept thinking, "It was an accident. I didn't do it on purpose."

From that moment on, I hated my mama. I hated her in a way that I'm almost embarrassed to admit now. I knew better than to ever disrespect her, but I didn't want to be in her presence either. Her words pierced the core of my soul. I am certain on that day my mama broke my spirit.

Please understand, I am not bashing my mama. She and I now have a very healthy relationship. Still, I need to tell my truth. My parents were young when my older sister and I were born. They were not ready to raise kids. They were still wrestling with their own demons. I get it. But that does not negate the fact that it negatively affected my life.

I cried all night because I was so heartbroken after that

incident. If I could have figured out a way to end my life that night without bringing reproach on my family, I would have. I walked the halls of school the next day like a zombie, barely present. I could always count on my band class to bring me joy. On that day, I wasn't so sure. I walked up the three steps leading into the band classroom and as soon as I lifted my head, I saw her. Alisha Baxter. Alisha was the drum major and a leader in her own right. I paid attention to her every move. I loved music and I loved band. She did too, but it all came natural for her. She was a singer and musician, as was her entire family. She could look at our sheet music and hear the music in her head and immediately play it. I, on the other hand, could not. I had to practice. I would stay up all night after everybody went to sleep and practice. But no doubt she and I would nail the parts the next day.

But this day was different. When I walked through the door of the classroom, it was as if a light was radiating from her. In hindsight, I really believe she was my guardian angel that day. She simply looked at me and smiled. That was the start of a beautiful sisterhood.

Alisha was my first real friend. She was the big sister I always wanted. I looked up to her. I am certain I would not have survived high school without her...or her family. I started staying with her every single weekend. I would go home with her on Fridays and come back to school with her on Mondays. I had no desire to be at home with my family. Alisha's home life was much calmer than mine. Her family wasn't perfect but they were stable. Her mom was the Pastor of a Full Gospel ministry in Warsaw, NC. I loved her church and in March of 1997, I gave my life to Christ.

Life didn't magically get better for me though. I still wrestled with spirits of rejection, depression, and sexual perversion. Why I chose not to totally surrender to God during this season of my life, I don't know. I had convinced myself that pretending to be okay was somehow an act of extreme faith, or at best, a sign of strength. I thought if I continued to press through my dysfunction and smile through my pain it meant I was being strong and courageous like the Bible says in *Joshua 1:7*.

The problem with this theory is it lacks authenticity. God isn't interested in who we pretend to be. He desires complete honesty and transparency from us. If "it" hurts, you gotta say it hurts. Not it stings. Not it's tender. Say, "it HURTS!"

While God is omniscient, it is still our responsibility to go to Him and make our requests known. I once heard a preacher say, "God can only heal what you reveal." I understand this logic, within context. Similarly to when we go to the doctor's office when we are experiencing "symptoms". The first thing the doctor asks is, "What is the problem?" or "Where does it hurt?" If you never confess that you are experiencing daily migraines, how will the doctor know how to help you? He can only heal what you reveal. God is our Chief Physician. So even if I couldn't tell those closest to me, I could tell God all about the pain I was in and allow him to heal me everywhere I was hurting.

Unfortunately, I was ignorant to that at the time. Therefore, I continued going downward on a very slippery slope.

I began dating a guy my sophomore year of high school and I guess you could say he was my high school sweetheart. (And I mean that in the most dysfunctional way possible, lol). I really liked him, but he just talked too much. He couldn't hold water with a bucket and that irritated me. Thanks to him, my good girl façade started fading quickly. We had a love hate relationship until our senior year of high school.

Our mutual friends would tell me I was so mean to him. I can't deny it, but they had no clue how annoying he could be at times. Or how he would share intimate details of our relationship with his friends during gym class. Our friends didn't seem to understand that the roar of my anger was my way of expressing the nonstop pain I was feeling. And to make matters worse, no matter how much I'd ask my boyfriend to keep his mouth shut, he wouldn't.

So, I secretly became more and more promiscuous. This was my way of not only hurting him but I was also punishing myself for being stupid and naïve years earlier. It was the only way I knew to numb the pain. I would meet older guys through a friend and I became a human dump truck. It was certainly my choice, but I hated it! When I think back I recall just how unfulfilled I was during this time in my life. I was hopping from bed to bed in search of SOMETHING. I wasn't sure what that something was at the time, but one thing is crystal clear to me now. I was looking for it in all the wrong places.

My searching left much of my senior year of high school in a blur. Without a doubt, God's hand of protection was on my life. Some of the dangerous and irresponsible things I did during this time of my life should have yielded catastrophic consequences, but God covered me. While I was consumed with doing my own thing, I still only had one main concern; graduating high school. I felt then and only then could I be free from all the drama, even the drama I had created for myself.

Over Christmas break during my senior year, I received my acceptance letter to the school of my dreams, Winston Salem State University. It was official, I was outta there! I was leaving Sampson County for good and I was NOT coming back. There was only one problem. I was pregnant. And I had no clue who the father was.

To say that I was distraught would be an understatement. To me, pregnancy meant I would be trapped and unable to live my dream of becoming a school teacher. I didn't know what to do. I cried almost every day for months because I could not believe I allowed myself to end up in such a predicament. Abortion wasn't an option for me. It just wasn't something I could bring myself to do. As I continued to hide my growing belly, I focused on my upcoming graduation with a fake smile permanently attached to my face.

However, one week before my graduation, everything changed. When I got to school, I was not feeling well. I had been feeling bad for quite some time, but I ignored it. By the time I got my first class I was in excruciating pain so I excused myself to the restroom. Once I got there, I realized I was bleeding profusely. I got help and someone called 911. My teacher seemed so afraid and kept asking if I wanted her to call my mother, but I told her no. By the time the ambulance arrived at the school, I was overwhelmed with shame. The paramedics were asking me so many questions.

"Miss Cole, did you know you were pregnant?"

"How far along are you?"

With my head hung low, I told them, "yes" I knew I was pregnant but I wasn't sure how far along I was because I had not sought prenatal care, not even once. The questions seemed to continue nonstop.

"How long have you been in pain?"

"Who is your doctor?"

The ride to the hospital was lonely, frightening, and embarrassing. The paramedics asked if I wanted them to notify my parents once I got to the hospital. In between my cries of pain and despair, I begged them not to call my mama. I was 18 years old, so they agreed, reluctantly. I didn't want my mama to find out the kind of life I had been living, especially not like that. Instead, I began to pray. I didn't know where to begin and I didn't know if God would hear my cry. So, I just prayed 5 simple words: **"I Just Wanna Be Free."** I wanted to be free from the shame of the rape. I wanted to be free from the wrath of my mama. I wanted to be free of the shame I had from disrespecting my own body. I wanted to be free from poverty. I wanted to be free from EVERYTHING that was holding me back and hindering me from reaching my full potential. I JUST WANTED TO BE FREE!!!!!

Once at the hospital, I was told I was having a miscarriage

and there was nothing they could do to save the pregnancy. After a few hours, I was released from the hospital and one of the administrators from my school took me home. On the way home though, I found out someone really did call my mama and told her I had been taken to the hospital. She worked out of town so by the time she got home, I was already there ready to tell her some ridiculous lie that I know she never believed. I didn't really care though, because not going to college was no longer a threat. And I couldn't have been more elated if I tried.

The following week, on May 26, 2000, I walked across the stage of Union High School as an honor graduate with my family cheering for me, as if nothing happened.

Two days later, I moved to Winston Salem, NC and I met Pastor Pamela Phillips (whom I affectionately call "Mom2") the following weekend while visiting her church. We clicked instantly. She was like a breath of fresh air to me. I had never met anyone so genuine, so pure hearted, and as transparent as her. She began to love on me immediately. She was the first person I truly opened up to and shared my heart with. Talking to her came so natural for me, probably because no matter what I shared with her, she never judged me or looked at me sideways. Over time, I knew she would be someone special, someone who would be a part of my life for a very long time.

Meanwhile, life on the campus of Winston Salem State

University was difficult. I had very few friends and I wasn't exactly social. I'd often skip classes and go to work instead because I was dirt broke and on my own. When I wasn't working, I was usually in church because I knew I was still broken. During my second semester, I tried singing in the Gospel Choir thinking maybe it would somehow fill the hole in my heart. It didn't. I just didn't quite fit in. For years, Winston Salem State University was all I ever talked about but I was so miserable there. So, after two and a half years, I dropped out.

And if that wasn't hard enough, my relationship with my mama was almost non-existent. I wasn't sure if she was jealous of the close relationship I had with my pastor, but weeks would go by and I wouldn't hear a word from her. My biological father received an early release from prison and lived about a mile from campus. I tried to develop a relationship with him, but he was so inconsistent. Looking back, I suppose we both were. But I felt he should have tried harder. His actions were the reason we were torn apart in the first place, not mine. He had a second chance to do right by me and my sister. He chose not to.

Yet another disappointment.

I don't think I realized back then how much not having my biological father present affected me. While I had the best substitute a girl could ever ask for, I believe that a piece of my heart was missing because deep down I never really knew who I was. And when you don't know who you are, you'll wander through life wounding whoever is in your path. At least, that's how things happened for me.

While I was secretly praying that things would turn around

for me, God was unbothered. In the midst of my pain, uncertainty, and unsurmountable guilt, He never doubted what He placed on the inside of me. God knew that one day my most earnest desire to be completely free would be manifested.

"I know what I am doing. I have it all planned out---plans to take care of you, not abandon you, plans to give you the future you hope for." Jeremiah 29:11 (MSG)

However, it was up to me to believe it.

4 WHY DID I GET MARRIED?

I've learned that you cannot make someone love you. All you can do is be someone who can be loved. I've learned that no matter how much I care, some people just don't care back... But it's not the end of the world.

~Iyanla Vanzant

If I had a dollar for every time someone asked me why I got married, I would be one wealthy woman. That's a question I have been asked more times than I can even count. When asked in times past, I would give a superficial response like, *"because it's better to marry than to burn."* *(1 Corinthians 7:9)* While there is some truth to that, it is not the real reason why I jumped the broom.

I could very well say, I was madly in love. I wanted companionship. I wanted a family. I desired an extra income. But none of those are the REAL reasons why I got married. Honestly, I was desperate and felt as if I needed a rescue.

If someone had told me that Kevin would eventually be my husband when I first met him, I would have called them a liar to their face. I wasn't the least bit attracted to him. He just wasn't my type. Despite that he caught my attention. He had the same slow, southern accent Reiny had and for some reason I was drawn to it. See, while we told everyone we met at our local library, the truth is, we initially met on a chat line. I was in my feelings one night, and the commercial came across my television so I dialed the number.

He and I chatted for a day or two, then decided to meet in person. In my mind, I'd have a one-night stand with him and then move on with my life. We met after hours, you guessed it, at our local library. When I saw him, I felt nothing. There was no chemistry between us whatsoever. That however, did not stop me from inviting him to my home and having my way with him. When it was over, I thought it was over. Only, he called me the next day wanting to hang out. I was caught all the way off guard!

He was sweet and sincere, so I played along. It didn't take long for me to realize he was a "yes" man. He rarely said no to me and would give me whatever I wanted. I equated his inability to say no as a sign of weakness, which was extremely unattractive to me. I used that weakness to my advantage by accepting and requesting countless gifts from him. Within a month of meeting, we were already talking about marriage. We'd lay in bed or chat over dinner, discussing our future together; all of the things we wanted for ourselves and as a couple. There was never a formal engagement. One day he showed up at my door with a ring and just slid it on my finger.

I proudly wore the ring, but deep down I was uncomfortable because I knew I was planning to marry someone who I was not physically attracted to, someone who began showing signs of dishonesty, and not to mention someone who I had only known for a month. But a week after our engagement, I found out I was pregnant. In my mind, that changed everything. Not getting married was no longer an option. I was the Youth Leader at my church so I had to be a good example for my youth group. Also, I was NOT going to be 23 and a single mother. No way, no how! That was out of the question.

In January of 2005 we began planning our wedding. We set our wedding date for May 21, 2005. I soon realized how stressful planning a wedding could be. Kevin and I seemed to argue about everything. I think he wanted a way out but was too scared to say it. Because I had the more dominate personality, I think he expected me to be the one to walk away. But I wasn't having it. I had too much at stake. I wasn't going anywhere. And neither was he.

Sometime in mid-February, I began having severe abdominal cramps and vaginal bleeding and had to be rushed to the Emergency Room. I was hemorrhaging. I immediately knew what was happening to me. I was miscarrying our child. The doctor told Kevin and me that I was experiencing an ectopic pregnancy and I would need to have a surgical procedure to completely terminate the pregnancy. It went well. But our relationship was never the same. Our shaky foundation began to crumble. He was heartbroken. I was numb. But we never talked about it. We just continued planning our wedding.

Some have asked why I continued to plan the wedding if I was no longer pregnant. Because, I had invested too much into this "event." I had already purchased a very expensive wedding gown. My girls had their dresses hanging in their closets. My mom had spent a lot of money as well. I ignored every reservation I had and marked my calendar until my wedding day.

Everything was happening so quickly with us. Our wedding day came almost as quickly as our engagement. When I woke up the morning of my wedding I was so excited. The day had finally come and I would finally become a married woman.

By the time I got to the church I was on Cloud Nine. I felt as if I was in a fairy tale - a real-life Cinderella story. I bounced around the church and my Pastor's Study like a young girl playing in the summer rain. Total and utter bliss. It's a feeling I can't quite explain. My family and friends were amazed by my excitement but what they didn't know was even in the midst of my enthusiasm, I was afraid Kevin wouldn't show up. My greatest fear was being stood up on my wedding day and being embarrassed in front of my family. For this reason, I refused to get dressed until I knew he was present and accounted for.

He didn't disappoint. Kevin showed up! I couldn't get in my wedding gown fast enough! Without hesitation, we exchanged vows and I was officially Mrs. Kevin K. Wilson.

Marriage is Ministry.

We've all heard that, right? I just wish I understood what it meant at the time. I didn't comprehend that marriage wasn't just about combined incomes, companionship, and legal sex. It's about supporting one another, loving each other through the good and the bad, believing in one another, and ministering to each other outside of the bedroom. And these things don't just happen overnight. It takes time, patience, and commitment. None of which, I had at the time. I was selfish and if things didn't go my way, I had no problem throwing a tantrum. I'd yell, scream, and cuss until he appeased me and met my demands.

I suppose that eventually began to annoy my husband. Three months into our marriage, he started working long hours and would only come home to sleep and shower. I hardly ever saw him anymore and that pissed me off! Our arguments began to escalate to full blown fights.

I remember our first fight so vividly. My husband didn't come home the night before and refused to tell me where he was. So, I began yanking all his clothes out of the closet and throwing them down the stairs. I was crying, screaming, and demanding that he leave and go back to where ever he stayed the night before. He looked me directly in my eyes and told me he wasn't going anywhere. Before I knew it, I had pushed him down our entire flight of stairs. It's a miracle he didn't break his neck, or something worse. Once I reached the bottom of the stairs, I was in a full-blown rage and before I could even consider an alternative I began punching, and kicking, and slapping him. I felt not coming home was the ultimate disrespect and I would not tolerate that in my home! And if he wasn't going to tell me where he was, then I'd beat it out of him. I, however, did not count on him fighting back. There we were, fighting like two boxers in a ring. We fought until we were physically exhausted. Then he gathered his clothes, got in his car and drove away. Once he was out of sight, I picked up my phone and called my mama. I didn't sign up for this. I wanted out!

By the time my mama picked up the phone, I was crying uncontrollably. I told her how Kevin didn't come home, how I thought he was having an affair, how we had just got into a fight and I made him leave. I told her everything. She let me cry it all out. When I was finished I waited for her to tell me I could come home.

After a few moments she said, "Tashia, stay with him."

Wait.

WHAT??????

"But Mama, whyyyy!!!!" I wailed. "You didn't stay!"

"Tashia, you are married!" She said firmly. "The first year is always the worst year. Y'all will get past this."

I was hurt and confused but I agreed to stay with my husband. After hanging up the phone, I sat in disbelief thinking, how did I get here? How did my life come to this? And what am I supposed to do now? I wasn't a violent person by nature. But I had allowed him to push me almost to the point of no return. Until that day, I had never experienced anger to that extreme. I realized if I didn't want to end up in jail, I would have to pull my emotions together.

My husband and I lived separately for a few weeks, although I saw him almost every Sunday at church and he continued paying the bills at home. I began to miss my husband tremendously, so he moved back home. For a while things were okay. Not good, not bad, just okay. We'd laugh. We'd fight. Then we'd makeup. Things were still shaky with us because we refused to communicate with each other. There was a lot of talking, yelling, and screaming but neither of us was truly listening. We were so busy trying to be right, that we failed to hear the heart of the person we had vowed to love and cherish until the day we took our last breath. In all the horrible and nasty words we said to each other, we were completely in error and outside of the will of God. Each danced to the beat of our own drum, we just continued downhill; full speed ahead.

Our marriage wasn't a real-life horror film. There were good times too. I can remember times when we would ride down I-40 laughing hysterically at his corny jokes, something that happened in church, or something so random. He brought out a side of me that I thought had died. There were moments when the little girl inside of me would raise up long enough to let me know that she was still in there; one single incident couldn't kill her. I'll always be grateful to Kevin for those moments. The problem though, was those moments were short lived and infrequent. I think that was because in my heart I knew my husband was having an affair.

Call it discernment or woman's intuition, but I knew without a shadow of a doubt there was another woman in the picture. He would still occasionally not come home. When he did, there would be scratches on his neck and back that did not come from me. But no matter how many times I asked him if there was someone else, he would deny it while professing his love for me. As a peace offering, he decided we should get away for the weekend. We didn't go far, but that mini vacation was probably the highlight of our entire marriage. We had so much fun. We laughed nonstop the entire weekend. We made love passionately and enjoyed each other's company. It felt like heaven on earth.

On the ride home, I asked him one last time if he was having an affair. I promised him I would not get angry or walk away from the marriage if he ended the relationship. (And I meant every word of it too) He told me he was not nor had he ever had an affair. I decided to believe him, because I was tired of fighting. I was finally ready to experience "happily ever after" with my husband.

For a whole two days, life was perfect. The atmosphere in our home shifted from hostility to peace, and I couldn't have been happier. But then, I received some devastating news over lunch shattering my hope of a fairytale ending for us. He told me his ex- girlfriend was pregnant.

"By who?" I asked as calmly as I could.

"She said it's mine."

Suddenly, I couldn't breathe. I felt like the walls were closing in on me. I felt weak. Like I was going to faint. I stood up slowly, and with tears streaming down my face, I walked away. I didn't say anything. I didn't yell, cuss, or scream. I just walked away.

Nine months later, his daughter was born and I was still by

his side. I wish I could say it was love alone that made me opt out of getting a divorce at that time, but it wasn't. It was desperation. I was so desperate for my marriage to work that I was willing to risk even looking foolish.

After things calmed down between us I accepted both his affair and his child. By this time, I had gotten my anger under control; had spent time gleaning from my Pastor. I was determined to make our marriage work. He didn't make it easy for me though. He would come home late with no explanation. He was mismanaging our finances. He blamed me for not being able to see his daughter. But I never fussed. I never argued because I knew that approach didn't work with him. I simply ignored his behavior and continued to shower him with love and affection.

But no matter how hard I tried, our marriage continued to fall apart. I tried to love him, support his decisions, and be there for him in every way possible. But nothing I did worked. He just didn't care anymore. No matter how much love I showed him, he would push me away. He had become mean and spiteful; just disrespectful. He was giving me back everything I had previously dished out to him—and that crap hurt! He would criticize my weight, my hair, the way I looked; even my inability to carry our child full term.

I am not sure if I resented him or if I just hated who I had become. Probably both. I was stressed out, emotionally drained, and heartbroken. I felt like I was two streets from crazy, but I just kept telling myself things would get better and eventually we would live happily ever after. But that day never came. How could it? We were two broken people trying to have a whole marriage.

I JUST WANNA BE FREE

Unfortunately, that's not how things work. When two broken people unite as one, chaos and dysfunction are to be expected. We both needed counseling but were too proud to admit it. So instead of attacking our problems, we attacked each other.

Police officers breaking down my front door, a restraining order, and a court date made me realize I had taken all that I was willing to take. I wanted out! I wanted to be free!

It would be so easy for me to blame him for everything and play the victim. Honestly, for years that is exactly what I did. But then I grew up, realizing I had to accept responsibility for the damage that I caused too. It wasn't his fault entirely. I was messed up before I married him. I wanted him to save me from myself and rescue me from all of my fears. That wasn't fair to him.

How was he supposed to save me? What made me think my husband had the power to rescue me? He wasn't God! He was just a man. A man with his own issues, his own insecurities, his own brokenness, and his own skeletons. That is why it is important to be honest with God because He is the only one who could have rescued me and saved me from myself.

I didn't know that then though. I felt the best way for us to heal and move forward with our lives was to end the marriage. I know God is not an advocate for divorce, but the safest thing for us to do was to separate. I wasn't sure where I wanted to go, but I knew I couldn't stay with him any longer.

On 9/11/07, I went to my mailbox and there it was, the

Dissolution of Marriage paperwork. I stared at the document not knowing how to feel. I was happy, and even a bit relieved. But I was still shattered. Embarrassed. And afraid. What would happen next? Would I survive the shame of a divorce after just 28 months of marriage?

Only time would tell.

5 THE STRUGGLE IS REAL

You can't say what you won't do. When you're broken, every touch feels like healing.

~Sarah Jakes

Being married then divorced made me tough. Real tough; even a little bitter. But I kept busy.

By the time 2008 rolled in, I was struggling in every area of my life, except financially. I was working for a very prestigious financial institution making more money than I had ever made in my life. But money isn't everything, especially when you have holes in your soul. Yes, I could shop in Lane Bryant anytime I wanted to or travel anywhere I wanted to, but acquiring "stuff" means nothing if your emotional and mental state needs healing.

I was scheduled to preach my initial sermon on January 20, 2008, the day after my 26th birthday. I needed to get away so the week prior I boarded Skybus Airlines and headed to Columbus, Ohio to spend some much-needed time to prepare for the next season of my life, preaching. I was there for 7 days and when I returned to North Carolina I was on fire for Jesus. Ready to slay any demon or demonic force daring to come my way. My initial sermon was a total success. My family came from near and far to support me and the gospel choir from my job sang for me. It was truly epic. "No More Jacob" was my sermon title from *Genesis 32:22-31*.

I talked about Jacob's defining moment, the moment when not only was his name changed, but so did his life. I knew all too well what he felt like because that's exactly where I was in my life. I didn't feel the need to deal with the hurt and pain I was feeling, but I decided I would move forward in the things of God.

It was during this season of my life when I became a callus Christian, leader, and minister. It was not intentional. I just hid it under the guise of being sold out to Christ. I was brutally honest and had no problem condemning folks to hell if I felt they just couldn't get it right and live 'holy.'

Let me be completely transparent, I was mean. I was arrogant. And I was self-righteous! I remember one of my co-workers balling her eyes out while telling me about an area of her life where she was struggling and how she just couldn't get a handle on it. Because she was a minister like I was, I felt she should know better. She should have been able to remove herself from any situation that challenged her faith or was contrary to the Word of God. I showed no mercy and would beat her over the head every chance I got with scriptures like, *"The wages of sin is death" (Romans 6:23).*

This went on for months.

But then the bottom fell out in my life. Suddenly I needed grace….and mercy (because there IS a difference). And for the first time, I knew what it felt like to need what I refused

I JUST WANNA BE FREE

to give to others. And it hurt...BADLY!

It all started with my love for music; all types of music. I pay attention to everything; the lyrics, the beat, the instruments, the harmony, everything! My immediate family and those closest to me had a hard time grasping the idea of a preacher who loved listening to secular music. My mama would say things, like "Oh so they play that song in church?" Because I wasn't strong enough to stand my ground, a lot of times I would just listen to the music when I was alone in my car.

One morning I pulled into the parking lot at work blasting, Natasha Bedingfield's song, "Love Like This" and parked my car beside my coworker and teammate who was blasting Joss Stone's "Put Your Hands On Me." We got out of our cars and began talking about music. We found out we shared the same love for "white girl music" as we called it. Natasha Bedingfield, Joss Stone, Amy Winehouse, and Fergie were a few of our favorites. Our love for music connected us. We quickly became close friends. We would go to plays, concerts, out to eat, to the movies-just everywhere. She even went with me to the dentist and held my hand while I got my tooth pulled.

This went on for months, us just hanging out. I enjoyed her company. She was fun. But most importantly, she allowed me to be myself. I didn't have to pretend with her. I could tell her about something that happened in church and then turn around a sing along to Fergie's "Clumsy" lyrics with her. She allowed me to be ME. No pretending, no holds barred.

But she was also a distraction. When we were together I didn't have to deal with the deep-rooted pain that was buried deep within my heart. I didn't have to deal with the freshness of my divorce and all of the confusing emotions that were attached to it. She represented freedom, an escape. And I loved every minute of it.

At some point our friendship began to evolve into something....else. I cannot pinpoint the exact moment when it happened but some way, somehow it did. I knew she was bisexual. She was very open about it, but when she had described her "type" in times past, it never resembled me so I assumed I was off limits.

I was wrong.

Seemingly with the snap of my fingers, things escalated and she and I became more than friends. Much more.

Almost immediately, I was addicted! Addicted far beyond a physical touch, as if there was an emotional tie to each of our souls. And it had me by the throat choking the life out of me. I knew what I felt was wrong. I knew what we were doing was wrong. But I didn't care, because for the first time in a long time I wasn't hurting anymore. The hole in my heart was closing in. I'd finally found a way to numb the pain (of a failed marriage, divorce, and unresolved childhood trauma) and go to sleep at night without crying. I even recall praying once, "God I need this! I'm willing to suffer the consequences later but for now, can I just enjoy this moment?"

Eventually I decided to tell my pastor what was going on with me, even though I knew she would likely be livid. So why tell her? Because I was her Ruth and she was my Naomi and you can't be that close to a person and keep secrets like that. And besides, while I did not want her help right then, I knew eventually I would need her prayers to help get me out. Because let's be clear, I was very much aware of how wrong it was. I knew it could never become a lifestyle for me. I knew it was very temporary.

When I told her, she was standing at her kitchen sink rinsing dishes. Her response was alarming, painful, yet not surprising. She looked me directly in my eyes and said, "Tashia, you know better! If you were my biological child, I would beat the crap outta you!" (and I believed her too). Her words hurt like nothing I had ever felt before, but I understood how she felt. I did know better. But she had no idea what it was like to desire the forbidden fruit.

In that moment, I learned a very valuable lesson. A person can KNOW better and not be able (or want) to DO better. Knowing right from wrong doesn't make you live right. Being delivered does. While I understood Pastor Pam's wrath, what I needed was healing and deliverance. I thought about this girl a lot more than I should have. There wasn't a day, a moment that went by when I wasn't thinking about her. I was fully aware that our souls were connected but had no clue how to break the chains. So, I settled. Because it was easier, and let's just be honest, my flesh was satisfied too.

For months, I indulged. And indulged. And indulged some more.

But after a while, it wasn't fun anymore. I soon realized

what I yearned for was far beyond anything she could ever give me. I thought I was craving her, but really it was my spirit crying out to be touched.

I needed and desired God in a REAL way. But how was I supposed to get to Him? Would He hear this sinner's confession/prayer? He knew it all. He knew every filthy thing I had done. That was done to me. I was too ashamed to go to God for myself, so instead I reached out to my peers in the Gospel.

One thing I can honestly say, of the few people who knew what I had fallen into, not one of them looked down on me or judged me. Pastor Pam's reaction was the harshest. And I knew what she said was said out of love. Everyone immediately went into prayer. Encouraging me. Reminding me that God still had need of me. I wasn't damaged goods. My life wasn't over. God was sure to get the glory out of my story. I appreciated it. But I didn't believe them.

Sometimes we beat up on ourselves so badly that we can't even receive love, hope, and wise counsel when God sends it. That is a very dangerous place to be in. It's dangerous because the devil wreaks havoc and has a field day in your mind. Tormenting you with your sin as if God could never forgive you. Well let me pause right here and encourage you, you are never too far gone! There is nothing you could possibly do that would make God love you any less than He already does. People may give up on you, you may even give up on yourself, but God will never leave you, neither will He forsake you. (*Deuteronomy 31:6*)

Remember my coworker who came to me crying uncontrollably because she could not seem to get a handle on her sin? The one I judged and refused to give the time of day? While our struggle was different, I realized what my coworker and I needed was the same: compassion, a listening ear, mercy, understanding, and truth without condemnation.

If you live long enough, life (and God) will humble you. And while right will always be right, and wrong will always be wrong- life isn't always easy. And the path isn't always clear. And sometimes, even when it IS, we still miss the mark. And we fall. And when we do, most of us just want a safe place to land. This is what my coworker needed from me. I know because that's what I was longing for when I told Pastor Pam and others of my misdeeds. I think most Christians aren't looking for someone to co-sign on their sin. I think they just need to know that they are not alone. They are not the first, nor will they be the last. Isn't that what we've all hoped and longed for after a fall? To be loved, having the reassurance that God would STILL forgive us if we repented. Knowing He would welcome us back into the flock, regardless of how it looked to others.

At some point, you have to move past the opinions of people and take the necessary steps to deliverance. And that takes courage, because pretending will never yield deliverance. True deliverance requires honesty. You have to be willing to be honest with yourself and with God. Then do the work!

I knew I had to make a decision. I could either continue down the path I was on. The path that made my flesh feel alive and vibrant but would surely lead me down the road of destruction or I could deny my flesh and allow God to heal me in every place I was hurting.

I chose healing.

Now I won't paint a rosy picture or insult your intelligence by making you think the deliverance process was easy, because it wasn't. I literally had to fight for it! There were many days when I doubted God's ability to deliver and set me free. On many occasions, I didn't think I was going to make it through the process. I wouldn't sleep for days at a time because I would be tormented in my sleep. Every time I closed my eyes I would hear keys jingling and a very sarcastic voice singing, "Latashiaaaaa" again and again. I was convinced it was the voice of Satan. I know without a shadow of a doubt he was literally trying to make me lose my mind, and quite frankly I almost did! My decision to live a holy and clean life was followed with downward spirals, a suicide attempt, unwanted visits to a psychiatrist, a diagnosis of Major Depressive Disorder, and mood stabilizing medication.

Hard to believe, isn't it? But trust me, I didn't plan on any of it either when I made the decision to be free.

One of my favorite movies is, "Things We Lost in the Fire," starring Halle Berry and Benicio Del Toro. In the powerful last scene, Benicio Del Toro's character is in a Narcotics Anonymous meeting and describes his recurring dream. The gist of what he says is this,

"I keep having this dream of me stealing silverware. Then I

sell it to a guy who owns a catering service. I go to buy drugs but my guy is not around. I go to other spots, but for some reason, no one is around. All of Seattle is dry. Then I get that feeling...of dread. And I panic, and I start crying. It's raining and it gets dark. Then I'm in my old apartment looking for something that I may have stashed away. I think I'm having a seizure...then I find some drugs that I have hidden in a suitcase. There I am with drugs in one hand and the money for my next fix in the other. And I feel at total, utter peace.

Then I wake up....

One day at a time. One day at a time. One day at a time. One day at a time."

The first time I saw that movie, I replayed that scene repeatedly and cried my eyes out each time. This described my struggle precisely. I understood what he felt in that moment. Knowing the very thing that's calming you is also the thing that's killing you. So, I adopted his philosophy. I decided to focus on one day at a time.

My prayer became, "Lord just let me get through the day without the urge to slip and tomorrow I'll start over again." I know that may seem strange (or elementary) but honestly it became too overwhelming to think any further ahead than that.

In addition to this new mindset, I also knew I had to sever all ties connected to my partner and the relationship. World renowned speaker and author, Joyce Meyer, has often said, "If you want to kill something, stop feeding it." Once I took her words seriously, I began to see the hand of God move in my life as I had never seen before. Everything that I thought would be a hindrance, God literally provided a way of escape. The phone calls and text messages came to a screeching halt. We went through a shift bid at work so our schedules changed, therefore we never saw each other.

I began to study and research every scripture and reference I could find relating to homosexuality, perversion, and sexual sins in general. I also got an accountability partner; someone I could reach out to if I ever felt weak without fear of being judged. These things helped me overcome my struggle.

I also believe these valuable tools can help you with any struggle you may be facing, whether it be drugs, alcoholism, gambling, pornography, whatever it may be. You have to decide that you are sick and tired of being sick and tired. Until then, you will continue to wallow in your sin and wrestle with your deliverance.

Trust me, that's not how you want to live. There is so much freedom on the other side of your struggle.

6 BEAUTY FOR ASHES

There is no shame in making mistakes while trying to figure things out. The goal is to live a fulfilling life, not a perfect one.

~Rob Hill, Sr.

Sometimes God will send you to a place you would have never chosen to go to teach you something you didn't know you needed to learn. My next season was full of uncomfortable but necessary transitions; I relocated to a new city and found a new church home.

The Tabernacle was everything I didn't want, but everything I needed at the time. Those folks were churchy and I wasn't used to that. But I liked it! Sadly, the excitement of a new atmosphere only lasted for about a year and a half. Then all hell broke loose again in my life.

My younger sister wanted to relocate and asked if she and my 2- year-old niece could move in with me. I immediately said yes. The bond I shared with the two of them is beyond comprehension. Saying no was never an option. She had lived with me briefly when I was married before deciding to return home. The only problem was, I couldn't bring myself to tell her I STILL had not gotten myself together.

She trusted me to get it together. However, I didn't fully consider how having two additional people to take care of would affect my finances. My sister was looking for a job, but other than seasonal work here and there she couldn't find anything to sustain my niece and herself. At one point, I worked two jobs to keep us afloat, but it was still a strain. We had what we needed (food, shelter, and clothing). But after a while, the laughter was gone. It was replaced with silent frustration. We never talked about it, but it was obvious. She was worried about how she was going to take care of herself and her child. I too was worried about how I was going to take care of myself, my sister, and her child. It was tough having two extra mouths to feed. I just wanted to be a positive role model for her, but I was failing miserably.

Soon she returned to our hometown. I knew she wasn't happy. She missed her life, her friends, and her old job. My niece's dad was trying to complicate things for her, so her leaving was inevitable. Still, I wasn't ready.

Three months after my sister left, I checked into High Point Regional Hospital-Behavioral Health. I just couldn't deal anymore. I had drifted into a hole that I couldn't dig my way out of. My Pastor recognized the warning signs and immediately took me to be evaluated. I wasn't quite suicidal but I had certainly lost the will to live. I couldn't bounce back. My house was so quiet after they left. There were no more footsteps running down the hallway yelling, "Aunt Ta-Ta." I missed them more than words could express.

Had I had the strength to activate the Word of God on the inside of me, I probably could have avoided this pain.

Instead, I was admitted and locked down for 72 hours before being released from the hospital. This caused a plethora of unpleasant events to follow. I lost my job and was evicted from my apartment. I ended up moving in with a church member for about a month until I could find another place to live. I did, but within 6 months I was evicted again. And that became my new cycle. Get a job. Lose the job. Get an apartment. Lose the apartment. Eventually no one else would rent to me, and I was officially homeless. After spending a few nights in various hotels, I moved into Leslie's House, a homeless shelter for women, in High Point, North Carolina. The thought of having to live in a homeless shelter was not only humiliating, it was also terrifying. However, I realized the people there were regular people just like me; there because of bad decisions or just down on their luck. You had your crazies here and there, but for the most part the people were okay.

The residents and staff loved me but they couldn't figure out why I was there. They kept asking me how I ended up there. I had no real answer to give them because I often wondered the same thing myself. I was a contract employee at a local bank and according to one of the staff members, I made more money than everyone in the shelter. While there, the staff showed me so much favor. They would always assign me the easiest chores to do and usually another house mate would do them for me. I rarely had to be in at our 6:00 PM curfew because they knew I was active at my church. I was even allowed to leave for a weekend to go on vacation to Washington, DC with two of my friends.

Yes, you read that correctly. I was homeless and still taking vacations. I literally toured Washington, DC for an entire weekend then returned to North Carolina and crawled into a bunk bed at a homeless shelter.

I know. Crazy, right?

Leslie's House was my home for about four months. They asked me to leave because my income was too high and they felt I could afford a place of my own. I left with garbage bags full of everything I owned. I didn't have a Plan B so I slept here, there, and everywhere. In an office at my church. On the floor of the daycare that my Pastor owned, hotels, and even at a friend's house once or twice. I never felt safe. Ever! From being followed to my hotel room to waking up in my church office next to a strange man sleeping only a few feet away from me.

This game of musical beds went on for about a year, until my best friend let me stay in her spare bedroom. I'd have to move an hour and a half away but at least I would be safe. I never told her I was homeless. I just asked if I could live with her for a little while. Without hesitation, she said yes and handed me the spare key to her home.

Seasons change. So of course, things finally started turning around for me. I had a great job with a great income, ready to get my own apartment again. The funny thing is, nobody in my life (except my Pastor and a few others) knew I was ever homeless, not even my immediate family. I kept in contact with them often enough so they wouldn't be alarmed…or pop in on me!

With the drama behind me, I was finally moving forward with my life. I launched my own mentoring program, "The beFree Foundation," for underprivileged and at-risk teen girls ages 13-19. I started this program to empower, embrace, and encourage the girls to "beFree to love the skin you're in." My mentorship increased to seven girls and I was progressing wonderfully!

Initially, I didn't pay much attention to my shortness of breath until a bad cough and chronic hoarseness started. I decided to see a doctor. After many tests that came back inconclusive, the doctors just assumed I had bronchitis or an upper respiratory infection. Weeks went by, but nothing relieved my symptoms. I continued to get worse. After a severe episode of shortness of breath, I went to the Emergency Room. The doctors found a large mass on my thyroid gland. While I was relieved to finally know the cause of my symptoms, I was advised to see my primary care physician right away. I immediately went into prayer as did those closest to me. My doctor told me I would need a biopsy to check for any signs of thyroid cancer.

Thyroid Cancer?

Did she just say, *"thyroid cancer?"*

Just hearing the word "cancer" made my heart skip a beat. I began researching the symptoms of thyroid cancer on the internet and found that I had every symptom listed. I braced myself for the worst possible outcome. When my doctor told me the news, I didn't flinch. I had been prepared without knowing it.

The report indicated I had papillary thyroid cancer and they were certain it had already spread to my lymph nodes. I immediately went into fight mode. I didn't have time to be scared. I just needed to know what the treatment plan would be. After more testing and failed treatments, I was diagnosed with Tall Cell Variant Papillary Thyroid Cancer, a more aggressive form of the cancer. I'd have to undergo a minimum of 5 weeks of radiation.

I was devastated, but I never showed it. I needed to figure out what the lesson was, because I had failed every test until then, and I didn't want to fail another one. I was tired of losing. Prayer, praise, and a positive attitude became my secret weapons. My support system was small in number, but mighty in strength.

When my faith would waver and I began asking, "what if" questions, they immediately reminded me what the Word says in *Isaiah 53:5, "...by His stripes we are healed."*

Once I dreamt of a woman whom I'd never seen before saying to me, "Tashia, you are not going to die. Although, there will be days when you will feel like it."

She was right.

Radiation was tough. It wasn't painful, but it was incredibly exhausting. It took a major toll on my body. Simple tasks such as getting out of bed for work and church was a challenge. On the days I could make it, I'd protect myself with nice clothes, a bright smile, and happy words. I secretly hoped somebody, anybody would notice I wasn't as resilient as I was pretending to be. No one ever did.

As my radiation treatments came to an end, I was so pleased with myself for remaining strong. Enduring months of treatment, complications, and medication without shedding a single tear was something I was proud of. On my last day of radiation, I left the Cancer Center full of joy, excited to never return. It was finally over. I practically skipped all the way to my car. I got in, turned my radio on full blast, and sang all the way home.

Once inside, I walked into my bathroom and looked in the mirror. However, I didn't recognize the woman staring back at me. I felt like such a fraud. I was grateful, but I was also exhausted. I was exhausted from the 5 weeks of radiation, but mostly I was exhausted from pretending.

So, I sat down on my bathtub, and for the first time since before the cancer diagnosis, I cried. I cried for every time I wanted to cry but told myself that would mean I was weak and didn't trust God. I cried for each time I walked out in the summer heat and my skin felt like it was on fire. I cried for the times when I was much too exhausted to go to work because I could barely lift my head up from my pillow. I cried for every time people who I thought loved me treated me indifferently because to them, I had the "good cancer" and that meant my journey should have been easier. I cried for the times when my hair became weak and brittle and I had to wear a wig.

I cried until I couldn't cry anymore. Then I got back in my car with my eyes almost swollen shut, drove off, and cried some more. This was the release I so desperately needed. God had healed me physically but this was bigger than thyroid cancer. It was bigger than being able to look back 10 years from now and being able to say I was a survivor. I needed to be healed emotionally, mentally, and spiritually.

I was at a point in my life where I knew I had to surrender it all. It wasn't easy because for over 20 years I thought I was a victim. I secretly blamed my bad behavior and poor choices on my biological father being absent, my rocky relationship with my mama, and on being raped as a child. While those things did affect my life, ultimately it was me who chose to live a reckless lifestyle.

My "mirror moment" (and all the other moments that followed) was enough to get my attention in a major way. It was that moment when I decided I didn't want to live another day in bondage. I knew if I wanted to fulfil the call of God on my life I had to deal with the root of my problems- shame; it overwhelmed me. The older I got, the more ashamed I became. I knew shame doesn't just pop up out of nowhere so I had to pinpoint its origination. What began as a little girl ashamed that her father was incarcerated, later turned into a preteen who blamed herself and was ashamed of being raped. Then came the shame of promiscuity, a failed marriage, homosexuality; then homelessness. I had done things that I said I would never do, only causing the shame to become more deeply rooted. But now it was time to deal with my issues head on and be free.

This epiphany made me realize the relevance of *Isaiah 61:3, which reminds us that God will "give them beauty for ashes."* It was as if God was saying, "Tashia, if you give me your ashes. I'll give you something beautiful." I knew I had been holding onto my ashes (pain, shame, guilt, filth) for far too long. Once I realized I could choose another path, I finally surrendered my ashes. I gave them all to

I JUST WANNA BE FREE

God, and this time, I didn't reach back for them.

In return, God gave me a beautiful testimony. Perhaps, not one I would have asked for, but nevertheless it's mine. And I don't have to be ashamed of it anymore because underneath my scars I've discovered a beautiful masterpiece.

I am now in a place where I can prayerfully help someone else not go down the road of destruction that I often found myself on. It is my desire for other women to know that no matter what you've done, you too can be free and receive beauty in exchange for your ashes.

7 FREE INDEED

You can take the mask off. You're safe now.

~God

When I first began writing this book, I was so afraid of what people would say or think if they knew the truth about me. Would they still love me? Would they judge me? Would they cast me away? But then I realized, there was nothing they could say about me that I had not already said about myself. They couldn't judge me any harsher than I had already judged myself. I decided to own my truth and let the chips fall where they may.

Yes, I realize I could have carried my secrets to my grave (and trust me, some I will lol), but I also knew I didn't go through everything I went through just for myself. Therefore, I had a responsibility to share my story and let other women know freedom is assessable to them just as it was for me.

I wish I could tell you I have all the answers, but I don't. No one journey is the same. So, instead I'll just tell you what has worked for me. I want to share four key principles that helped me on my journey to freedom that I believe will be beneficial to you as well.

1: Stop Making Excuses.

There is a parable in the Bible in *John 5: 1-15* where there is a man laying at the Pool of Bethesda. He has been lame and cripple for 38 years and he's at the pool waiting for someone to put him in the water so he can be healed. Jesus appears and asks him a question, "Do you want to be made well?" The man answered Him, "Sir, I have no man to put me into the pool when the water is stirred up; but while I am coming, another steps down before me."

No matter how many times I've read this story I always pondered the same question; why didn't the man just say, "Yes! I want to be healed?!?!" He had been lame for almost 40 years! But instead of screaming the true desire of his heart to the one person who had the ability to meet his need, he offered an excuse. I would read this parable while shaking my head in disgust, until I realized I was guilty of doing the same thing. Over the years, I had decided countless times that I was ready to be free. But the truth is, a part of me was comfortable being in bondage. I had somehow grown accustomed to my chains because they provided a certain level of safety and security. So, I made one excuse after another.

I had to learn just as you cannot serve two masters, you can't have both freedom and bondage at the same time. Not if you desire to live in the fullness and the overflow of God. It just doesn't work like that.

Excuses will only take you so far, which really isn't that far at all. So, until you stop making excuses you will continue to watch everyone else around you receive the very thing that you need. At some point, you must ask yourself, "how bad do I want it....and what am I willing to sacrifice to get it?"

2: Forgive Yourself.

There was a time in my life when of Jesus' twelve disciples, I would often compare myself to Judas. I know, odd choice isn't it seeing how he is considered the bad apple in the bunch. But it's not the betrayal of Judas that I can most relate to. It is the devastation of a decision that he couldn't fix that tugged at my heart the most. I knew the agony that comes with making a poor decision and wishing you could go back and change it. Perhaps, like me, you have done things you are not proud of or hurt someone and wish you hadn't. Many of us can reflect over our lives and find something that makes us ask… "What was I thinking?"

Judas made a horrible mistake. One he tried to correct, but it was too late. The damage was done. Was he wrong? Absolutely! But nobody is perfect. We've all been somebody's disappointment at one time or another. But your destiny does not have to be like that of Judas'. You don't have to forfeit your future because of one (or several) bad decisions.

Instead, you can learn to forgive yourself and make peace with the shattered pieces. Judas chose to end his life rather than forgive himself for his wrongdoing. That was ALMOST my story too, but thanks be unto God it's not!

Moreover, it doesn't have to be your story either. Unfortunately, life doesn't come with a reset button. There are no do-overs. However, you can decide today to forgive yourself and move forward committing to do better.

3: Take Time to Heal.

Let me ask you something, have you ever seen a football player break his leg mid game then jump up and run the next play? Of course, you haven't! Why? Because healing is important. If you desire to be effective and able to operate at your highest potential, you must take time to heal.

What am I saying? You must take a step back and access the damage that has been done to your mind, body, and soul. I know it's easier to dance around your issues and pretend like "it" didn't happen. But listen to me clearly, you'll never grow by hiding, or lying either. There were times when I wanted to pretend like the bulk of my life never happened. I never wanted to be a 25-year-old divorcee who was struggling with her identity. That wasn't a part of the script I had written out for my life. But whether I wanted to accept it or not, it became my truth, my reality. And I had a responsibility to own it, make peace with it, and choose to heal! So, my question to you is, are you sick and tired of being sick and tired?

If you are, then it is time to start your healing process. God can heal you in every place where you are hurting. Are you broken? Do you blame yourself for the abuse you endured as a child? Are you harboring unforgiveness in your heart? Whatever it is, give it to God, the only One who can heal and restore you.

The process of healing and restoration takes time. Some wounds are more painful and more deeply rooted than others, so don't expect a hasty path to becoming whole again. Take as much time as you need. If you need to reach out to a third party for additional support (such as a counselor, therapist, or mentor), then do that! Get free by any means necessary!

4: Be Your Own Rescue.

I told you I got married because I wanted my husband to be my rescue. When he and I met, I was broken and expected him to fix everything that was wrong with me. I wanted him to make me feel whole, worthy, and loved. But instead I left the marriage feeling ten times worse than when I entered. That's because I failed to understand the importance of being my own rescue. Author and Transformation Coach, Lisa Nichols says, "Everything you need to get back up is already inside of you..." When I heard those words, it was as if my spirit leaped. Her words arrested my life and catapulted me toward my destiny. I knew at that moment, I wasn't passing out anymore invitations to my own pity party.

I took what she said even a step further and noted—the reason why I already have everything I need is because God gave it me, He placed it on the inside of me. According to *2 Peter 1:3*, God *"...has given to us all things that pertain to life and godliness."*

I only needed to activate it.

Which meant, I didn't have to wait on anyone to give me permission to be free or to be my authentic self. I just needed to wake up every day and choose victory over defeat, forward movement over stagnation, forgiveness over hatred, and freedom over bondage. And that is exactly what I did!

I have since learned that pain produces both power and purpose. When you get sick and tired of being pitiful, you'll start kicking your way out of your situation and rise to the occasion. You'll reach deep within yourself and pull out the warrior, the lioness; the winner that was begging to come forth all along. Because the truth is, we ALL have secrets and skeletons in the closet. The key though, is not allowing them to define who you are or determine how far you will go in life.

The moment my life changed in 1994, I wanted nothing more than to feel safe again. But instead I encountered one tragedy, one mishap after another. For years, I'd ask "Lord, why me?" I asked that question so much I'm sure God was like, "Girl, just chill. I got you!" I never knew how much God "had me" until my healing process began. It was only then that I recognized I was living with gaping wounds that just continued to bleed all over those around me. I now know that my surrendered "yes" (to God's plan) saved my life.

I am not sure what God has in store for me in the days,

months, or years to come. I could travel the world and minister to thousands upon thousands of lost souls, or I may never leave North Carolina. However, one thing is for certain, I won't be in bondage while I wait. I won't second guess whether God loves or forgives me. I won't dumb down the anointing of God that rests on my life. I won't wonder if there was purpose behind all the pain I've endured.

I just believe that no matter what I've done in my past, I still deserve to live a fruitful and productive life (and so do you).

My minister friends were right. God CAN still use me. He CAN still get the glory out of my story. And I CAN walk authentically and unapologetically in my freedom, knowing *that "if the Son makes you free, you shall be free indeed." (John 8:36)*

And I'm free, baby!

Prayer of Salvation:

For it is with your heart that you believe and are justified, and it is with your mouth that you profess your faith and are saved. As Scripture says, "Anyone who believes in him will never be put to shame…. For, "everyone who calls on the name of the Lord will be saved." (Romans 10:9-10, 13) NIV

I am not sure of your spiritual condition; maybe you were blessed with this book by a loved one or perhaps you picked it up because you've hit rock bottom. The promises of God are for the believer so let me walk you through the plan of salvation. Surrendering your life to God and your heart to Christ will be the best decision of your life. Repeat after me…

Heavenly Father, I come to You admitting that I am a sinner. I choose to turn away from sin, and I ask You to cleanse me of all unrighteousness. I believe Jesus rose from the dead so that I may be justified and made righteous through faith in Him. I call upon the name of Jesus Christ to be the Savior and Lord of my life. I declare right now, I am a born-again child of God. I am free from sin and full of the righteousness of God. I am saved in Jesus' name. Amen.

What Does the Bible Say About?

(NIV recommended translation)

Deliverance

Psalm 34:19

Psalm 91:15-16

Isaiah 42:16

Proverbs 28:26

Spirit of Rejection

Isaiah 41: 9-10

Deuteronomy 7:6

2 Thessalonians 2:13

1 Sam 12:22

Letting Go of the Past

Ephesians 4: 31-32

Isaiah 43: 18-19

2 Corinthians 5:17

I Say a Prayer…

I pray that every spirit of pain, brokenness, sickness, loneliness, and insecurity be broken off of you. I pray for anyone who has to cry themselves to sleep tonight be comforted. I pray for any of you who have had to make decisions that were unpleasing to God- but feel you had to do what you had to do. I pray for peace, for healing, and for restoration. I pray for everyone's family who have generational curses of physical abuse, sexual abuse, poverty, mental illness, infidelity, divorce, addictions, and afflictions. To anyone who feels no one values them, to anyone who feels their mama didn't love them right, or their daddy wasn't around and now feel they have to settle for half-truths and false idols, I say a special prayer for you.

For all who have watched a loved one fight cancer--but consequently lose the battle...for those who have (or may know someone with) HIV/AIDS because of that ONE time...for all who had moments where they didn't know if they would see one more day, I pray for you! For those who are (or have been) confused about their sexuality and hate themselves...guess what, God STILL loves you! Please, don't believe the lies!

Lord, mend these broken hearts. Allow them to learn from the sins and mistakes of others so they can travel a different path. Lord, I am not claiming to know the Bible from Genesis to Revelations-- but Lord I know YOU and I pray for anyone who is unsure will find the courage to seek you too.

For anyone who has lost faith, strength or hope...you can

borrow mine!!! Hold on for one more day, then tomorrow---hold on for another one.

Despite how you may feel--Try Jesus! I know it sounds like a cliché but I'm telling you--if you try Him, your life will NEVER be the same!

I love you all. May God bless and keep each and every one of you!

Acknowledgements

I'm indebted to quite a few folks who have not only hung in there with me during the long process of writing of this book but for those who just did LIFE with me! OMG, I am so thankful. First and foremost: I thank God for being who He is to me. In Him do I live, move, and have my being. Without Him I am NOTHING and can do NOTHING.

Many, many thanks to my friends and to my entire family. More specifically I'd like to thank...

Mama: Lord knows we have had our share of challenges but we overcame them all, together. You've always supported my decisions, dreams, and goals no matter how crazy they sounded. Well, except when I said I was moving to Richmond, VA. Lol you were NOT having it! God worked it out though, didn't He?

LaShondria: My little big sis. My first friend. Your resilience and tenacity has been a point of reference for me during some of my most difficult storms. Thank you for being such an amazing example of what strength looks like.

LaDeidra: There really should be a law prohibiting us from being anywhere together that requires us to be serious. You are the only person in the world who makes me laugh until I throw up! Remember when....? Well, never mind! Lol. I've always said you are the best little sister a girl could ask for. I mean it, too! I love you, girl.

Pastor Pamela Phillips (Word of Truth Int'l Life Center Winston Salem NC): (whom I affectionately call

"Mom2"): Thank you for your unwavering love, patience, sacrifices, and for not ignoring the call of God on my life, regardless of how ratchet I was at times. I didn't make it easy for you but know I am who I am because of your guidance, tutelage, and wise counsel. "There is no way I can pay you back, but the plan is to show you that I understand. You are appreciated." ☺

Pastor Barbara Battles (The Greater Power and Praise Tabernacle, High Point NC): Thank you for saving my life, in more ways than one.

Minister Cheryl Jeffries: You were the first person to confirm that I would become a published author. I know God placed you in my life to make sure I would live to see the prophecy fulfilled. You prayed me through some rough times; never judging, never condemning. I am forever grateful.

Crystal Ervin: I am a better person because of your friendship. You pushed me to birth this book in more ways than you could ever imagine. Thank you!

Tramika Craddock: Believe it or not, because you had the courage to take a leap of faith and do what you were called to do, it gave me the courage to do the same. Thank you for JUMPING!

Bridgett Battles: Thank you for the random phone calls and advice. I bet I can give you my elevator speech now! Ask me again!

Cassandra D. Watts: You are hands down the best editor on this side of heaven! The first round of edits had me wanting to literally throw my entire manuscript in the trash, but the moment you told me that I was going to have to really push myself, I knew you were the right person for the job. Thank you for believing in me and for reminding me that my story was worth sharing.

Lastly but certainly not least,

Orienthia Speakman (My Mentor, Transformation Coach, and Spiritual Mother): In my pursuit of authentic relationships, I met you. It felt like God just dropped you out of the sky and right in my pathway. We've since shared so many destiny moments. You were certainly the Pitocin to this labor process; and that annoyed and angered me in ways that now makes me laugh hysterically. Because of you, I have finally birthed my masterpiece. Thank you, Mama O!

ABOUT THE AUTHOR

Latashia Renee is a woman of virtue, poise, and integrity. She is a dynamic teacher, preacher, administrator, and atmosphere shifter. Her passion is ministering to women and young adults who are broken, by assisting them in achieving spiritual and emotional healing. Latashia's testimony reassures others that God is a healer, a deliverer, and a mind regulator. When she is not writing, she enjoys laughing every chance she gets, shopping, and spending time with family and friends. She currently resides in North Carolina.

Made in the USA
Middletown, DE
30 September 2023

39478071R00050